D0903253

COLIN

POWELL

Military Heroes

COLIN POWELL

GENERAL & STATESMAN

by Sue Vander Hook

Content Consultant:
Dr. Clarence Lusane
Associate Professor, American University

ABDO
Publishing Company

CREDITS

Printed in the United States of America,
North Mankato, Minnesota
102009
012010

 PRINTED ON RECYCLED PAPER

Editor: Mari Kesselring
Copy Editor: Paula Lewis
Interior Design and Production: Emily Love
Cover Design: Emily Love

Library of Congress Cataloging-in-Publication Data
Vander Hook, Sue, 1949-
  Colin Powell : general & statesman / Sue Vander Hook.
     p. cm. — (Military heroes)
  Includes bibliographical references and index.
  ISBN 978-1-60453-965-3
  1. Powell, Colin L.—Juvenile literature. 2. Statesmen—United States—Biography—Juvenile literature. 3. African American generals—Biography—Juvenile literature. 4. Generals—United States—Biography—Juvenile literature. 5. United States. Army—Biography—Juvenile literature. I. Title.
  E840.5.P68V36 2010
  973.931'092—dc22
  [B]
                                    2009032364

TABLE OF CONTENTS

Colin Powell in Vietnam

HUEY DOWN

ajor Colin Powell arrived at Duc Pho, Vietnam, on July 27, 1968, to perform his second tour of duty. It had been the deadliest year yet in the Vietnam War. More than 1,000 U.S. troops had been killed each month.

Powell's assignment was to prepare the Eleventh Infantry Brigade for annual inspection. His duties were mostly administrative, but before the end of the year, he would face a near-death experience. He would also perform a deed that made him worthy of the Soldier's Medal.

Rare Victory

Major General Charles M. Gettys was commanding officer of the Eleventh Infantry. In November 1968, Gettys needed a temporary officer of operations and planning. He had read good things about Powell in the *Army Times*, an independent military newspaper. Gettys appointed Powell to the important position. Powell went from preparing 800 men for inspection to planning combat strategy for 18,000 troops and 450 helicopters.

Powell's new position took him to Chu Lai, the large U.S. military headquarters on the east coast of South Vietnam. On Friday, November 15, 1968, he and the troops had reason to celebrate. Members of the Eleventh Infantry had achieved a decisive victory. They had discovered 29 enemy camps that day and seized a huge North Vietnamese Army weapons cache. General Gettys wanted to see the spoils for

Little City

Chu Lai operated from 1965 to 1971 as head-quarters for the U.S. armed forces in Vietnam. Its large airfield provided the main way in and out of Vietnam for the majority of U.S. troops. Abundant military housing, stores, post offices, churches, officers' clubs, and more gave Chu Lai the appearance of a small, thriving city.

himself. The next day, he and Powell, along with seven others, boarded a UH-1H Iroquois helicopter—commonly called a "Huey."

The mood was festive inside the chopper. Clear-cut victories were rare in this difficult and unpopular war. The Eleventh Infantry had just scored big. The pilot of the helicopter, Chief Warrant Officer James D. Hannan, flew the loaded Huey west over steep hills covered with dense jungles. On the ground, a U.S. Army battalion commander ordered his men to clear a landing in the middle of the thick jungle. When the Huey approached the site, ground troops set off a smoke grenade to mark the spot where it could land safely.

Landing a helicopter on such a small area in the middle of thick vegetation was not easy. The hole in the jungle was just wide enough to accommodate the diameter of the main rotor. Hannan approached the site at a fast speed and then aborted the attempt to lower the chopper. He tried a second time. He hovered over the site before slowly and carefully lowering the aircraft. The rotors chopped up

A Huey helicopter

branches on the way down, sending debris whirling into the air. Powell, who could see what was happening, shouted, "Pull out!"[1] The warning came too late. Hannan was already fighting to maintain control of the Huey. A fierce backdraft pushed the rotor into a tree, stopping the blades immediately. From approximately the height of a three-story building, the chopper began to free-fall.

Huey Down

As the chopper fell, Powell put his head down and locked his arms around his knees—he assumed the crash position. The Huey hit the ground.

After impact, Powell quickly unfastened his seat belt, jumped out of the chopper, and ran from the site. That is what soldiers were trained to do—get away from the crash before the craft could catch fire. But then Powell and Private First Class Bob Pyle turned around to look at the smoke-filled wreck. Some members of their group were still in the helicopter. Powell and Pyle made their way back to the wreck and began prying, pulling, and unfastening seat belts. Their trapped comrades

The Vietnam War

The Vietnam War was the longest war in U.S. history. It lasted from 1959 to 1975. The first conflicts began over the French colonial rule of Vietnam. At first, the United States aided the French in keeping Vietnam a colony. But by the mid-1950s, Vietnam had gained independence from France, and North Vietnam was under communist control. The communists wanted to make North and South Vietnam into one communist nation in which property is shared in common and individual freedoms are limited to benefit the state.

By 1959, the United States had sent military advisers to South Vietnam to help prevent a communist takeover. In 1965, the United States deployed its first combat troops to South Vietnam. During the next two years, 500,000 troops were deployed to South Vietnam. Fighting continued until 1975, when U.S. efforts to stop communism failed. When North Vietnam captured Saigon, South Vietnam came under communist control. On April 23, 1975, President Gerald Ford declared an official end to the Vietnam War. By April 30, all U.S. troops were home. In 1976, a unified Vietnam was officially named the Socialist Republic of Vietnam.

The cost of the war was high for the United States as well as Vietnam. More than 58,000 Americans lost their lives. Between 2 million and 4 million Vietnamese were killed.

appeared to be either unconscious or dead. Powell first pulled out General Gettys, whose shoulder was bent at a strange angle. Powell dragged him into the woods. Several soldiers on the ground joined in the rescue effort.

Powell, Pyle, and other rescuers ran back to the wreckage to free Colonel Jack Treadwell, Gettys's chief of staff. With help, Pyle removed the pilot from the aircraft. Then, Powell and the other men turned to help Captain Ron Tumelson, who was

The Huey

The UH-1H Iroquois (Huey) is a single-engine U.S. Army helicopter that became well known for its service in the Vietnam War. It was equipped with instruments for flying at night and in poor weather. In place of wheels, the Huey had skids, which allowed it to land on swampy or bumpy land. During the Vietnam War, approximately 2,500 Hueys were shot down, resulting in the deaths of more than 2,200 U.S. pilots.

also trapped. Powell thought Tumelson was dead, but then the injured soldier groaned. The men were able to get him out of the Huey and into the woods. Powell's group suffered plenty of injuries that day. The pilot had the worst—a broken back—but at least they all were alive.

Overhead, a throng of U.S. Army helicopters seemed to appear from nowhere. The army had received news of the crash and reacted quickly. One of the choppers was a dust-off bird, a medical evacuation helicopter called a MEDVAC for short.

The Soldier's Medal

The Soldier's Medal was created by the U.S. Congress on July 2, 1926. It is awarded to anyone in the army who shows acts of extreme bravery in a situation that does not involve conflict with an enemy.

It was equipped with a winch and cable that pulled each of the injured up and into the helicopter.

The MEDVAC then flew to the army base hospital at Chu Lai. Gettys's arm was put in a sling to immobilize his broken shoulder. Powell's X-rays showed a broken bone in his ankle, and he was fitted with a cast. It would take seven years for his injury to heal completely.

BRAVERY REWARDED

For his acts of heroism in saving the lives of his fellow soldiers, Colin Powell was awarded the prestigious Soldier's Medal. But that day for Powell was just the beginning of an impressive military and political career and a lifetime of remarkable achievements. He would become a four-star general, chairman of the Joint Chiefs of Staff, and U.S. secretary of state. He would serve in three wars, oversee numerous military conflicts, and hold government positions under nine U.S. presidents. Colin Powell would become one of the most respected U.S. generals and statesmen of all time.

Powell visited the Vietnam Veterans Memorial in 1991.

Colin's mother, Maud Ariel "Arie" McKoy

GROWING UP
IN NEW YORK

Colin Powell was born April 5, 1937, in Harlem. It was a largely African-American neighborhood in the New York City borough of Manhattan. Both of Colin's parents had emigrated there from Jamaica in the 1920s.

Colin's father, Luther Theophilus Powell, grew up in southwestern Jamaica. He was the second of nine children in a very poor family. Luther never graduated from high school and worked in a store as a young man. In his early twenties, he boarded a banana boat and came to the United States.

Colin's mother, Maud Ariel "Arie" McKoy, was born in western Jamaica in Westmoreland. She was the oldest of nine children in a family with somewhat higher social status than Luther's. Arie graduated from high school and then found clerical work in a law office. But soon Arie's mother left home, possibly because of her husband's drinking habit. Arie's mother searched for work in Panama, Cuba, and finally the United States. In time, Arie joined her mother in New York City.

HOMETOWN: HARLEM

Luther and Arie met in New York City. In 1929, they were married at St. Philip's Church in the heart of Harlem. The Harlem Renaissance was in full swing. African Americans

Jamaican Roots

In 1961, at the age of 24, Colin Powell made his first trip to Jamaica. This was where both of his parents were raised and where many of his relatives still lived. When he arrived, his relatives welcomed him with open arms. Colin wrote, "I was suddenly drenched in sunlight, surrounded by lush flowers, and enveloped by aunts, uncles, and cousins who took me in as if they had known me all my life."[1]

freely expressed themselves in art, music, and literature. Talent and entertainment overflowed from clubs that swayed to the beat of jazz and blues. Magazines and newspapers were packed with African-American literature and poetry by writers such as Langston Hughes and Countee Cullen.

Black Americans were drawn to the excitement and the opportunities that Harlem offered. Thousands had migrated there to find jobs in the industrial North. Some had come from the South,

The Harlem Renaissance

The Harlem Renaissance was a blossoming of African-American culture during the 1920s and 1930s. In 1925, African-American writer and professor Alain Locke coined the term "Harlem Renaissance" in his anthology *The New Negro*. He summed up the movement, saying that through art, "Negro life is seizing its first chances for group expression and self determination."[2]

The economy was booming in the 1920s. Approximately 750,000 African Americans were pushed out of the South due to racist attitudes. They went to the North to find a better life. This was called the Great Migration. Approximately 175,000 of the African Americans settled in Harlem, a three-square-mile (7.8-sq-km) area in New York City.

African-American musicians, writers, and artists flourished in Harlem. Jazz was heard nightly at places such as the Apollo Theater and the Cotton Club. The music of Duke Ellington, Count Basie, and others was performed to packed crowds. Writers such as Langston Hughes unleashed their creativity. Visual artists such as Jacob Lawrence used vivid colors and interesting shapes to depict the struggles that African Americans had endured.

The Harlem Renaissance faded away in the mid-1930s. It ended most likely because of the hard economic times of the Great Depression and growing racial tensions in the area.

others from islands in the West Indies, such as Jamaica, Trinidad, and Barbados.

Luther and Arie both had jobs in Manhattan's garment district. Luther worked in the shipping department at Ginsburg's, a manufacturer of women's clothing. He was a loyal worker who would stay with the company for 23 years. He began as a stockroom clerk and eventually moved up to foreman of the shipping department. Luther stood only five feet two inches (157 cm) tall, but his work ethic, determination, and kindness made up for any lack of height. Arie, a plump, petite woman, did her work at home. Each night at the kitchen table, she sewed buttons and trim on garments. It was piecework—instead of being paid by the hour, Arie was paid for each item of clothing she completed.

The Powells' first child, Marilyn, was born in 1931. Five and one-half years later, they had a second child—Colin Luther. By then, Harlem was a different place. The United States was in its seventh year of the Great Depression. Unemployment was high and incomes were low. The splendor of the Harlem Renaissance was gone. Crime and drugs were taking the place of arts and entertainment.

"BANANA KELLY" NEIGHBORHOOD

In 1943, when Colin was six years old, his parents did what many other families were doing. They left Harlem and moved across the Harlem River to the South Bronx. It was a safer place at that time to raise a family. The South Bronx was densely populated with a variety of cultures—Jewish, African-American, Italian, Polish, Hispanic, and more. Everyone lived close to each other in two- to four-story brick tenements. The Powells moved into a roomy, four-bedroom, third-floor apartment at 952 Kelly Street.

New York City was crowded, busy, and sometimes dangerous. But Colin did not notice how huge or overwhelming it was. His world was his neighborhood, where his aunts, uncles, close friends, and godmother lived. His world was Kelly Street, curved just right to earn the nickname "Banana Kelly."

Colin's neighborhood had just about anything a person needed. Grocery stores, department stores, pharmacies, and bakeries lined the streets

The Great Depression

Beginning in the early 1930s, the United States was plunged into severe unemployment and poverty in a period known as the Great Depression. By 1937, the year Colin Powell was born, the economy was beginning to recover. Colin's parents were fortunate to have jobs during the Great Depression.

Colin at age five

along with candy shops, shoemakers, and movie theaters. A busy elevated train line was at the end of Colin's block. Every day, trains rumbled through, shaking the neighborhood. Colin grew used to their clanking wheels and squealing brakes. He liked nearly everything his crowded borough and urban neighborhood had to offer. He would later write, "The South Bronx was an exciting place when I was growing up, and I have never longed for those elms and picket fences."[3]

SCHOOL DAYS

Colin's elementary school—a public school designated PS 39—was just three blocks from his home. His junior high school was one block farther. Between the two schools was St. Margaret's Episcopal Church, where the Powells worshipped on Sundays.

Colin did not do well in school. By the fourth grade, he was placed in a class for struggling students. He was not very good at sports, either. As hard as he tried, even under the hopeful eye of his father, he rarely connected a bat to a ball. Music lessons—in piano and flute—also proved unsuccessful.

Colin's sister, Marilyn, on the other hand, was bright and talented. She seemed to succeed at everything she tried. Growing up in her shadow could have discouraged Colin. But he was a happy child who enjoyed life immensely. When he was not in school, he played with friends. Color or background did not matter

CAH-lin or COH-lin?

When Colin Powell was four years old, his friends changed the way they pronounced his name. It had been CAH-lin, a British-Jamaican pronunciation. But at the end of 1941, when the United States entered World War II, he became COH-lin. A World War II pilot named Colin P. Kelly Jr. had just become a war hero. His plane had been shot down two days after the Japanese attack on Pearl Harbor. Everyone was talking about Colin (COH-lin) Kelly, who had sacrificed his life so his crew could bail out of the plane. In time, Powell became COH-lin of Kelly Street. His family, however, still called him CAH-lin. Today, Powell prefers to be called COH-lin.

to the neighborhood boys. They were all buddies. Whether they were on a porch, a street, or an empty lot, the boys came up with a game to play.

In junior high school, Colin's grades improved somewhat. Then, in 1950, he entered high school. Marilyn had attended Walton High School, one of the elite schools for high-achieving students. Colin wanted to go to Stuyvesant High, another prestigious school, but his guidance counselor would not give him a recommendation. Colin attended Morris High School, which had no special requirements for admittance.

Average Student

Colin's high school grades were average. He admitted that he lacked direction and nothing fired him up. But he did stay out of trouble. In an area where drugs and crime were growing, Colin avoided illegal activities. His part-time job probably kept him out of trouble. When he was 14, he started working at Sickser's, a neighborhood store that sold baby furnishings and toys. He was a hard worker. At the end of Colin's first day, store owner Jay Sickser recognized that. "So you're a worker," Sickser told him. "You want to come back tomorrow?"[4]

And Colin did go back. He worked for Sickser throughout his high school years. The young man developed a strong work ethic and learned some Yiddish along the way from the store's many Jewish customers.

Colin graduated from Morris High School in 1953 with a C average. His father expected his son to attend college. Even though Luther had never graduated from high school himself, he knew the importance of a good education. He told his children that education was the key to success.

Searching for a College

To please his parents, Colin set out to find a college that would accept him. To his surprise, he was accepted at two colleges: New York University (NYU) and City College of New York (CCNY). Tuition at NYU, a private college, was $750 a year. It was $10 at CCNY, a public school that had been established for working-class citizens' children. Colin chose CCNY. It was not a huge university or an elite private college. There, Colin would find something he really liked and could excel at.

*Colin's father, Luther Theophilus Powell, encouraged
his children to pursue good educations.*

Powell wearing his ROTC uniform in 1954

An Army Career

In February 1954, 16-year-old Colin Powell boarded a city bus in the Bronx. He headed to Harlem for his first day of classes at the City College of New York (CCNY). He did not really want to go to college. He later admitted, "I went to college for a single reason: My parents expected it. I don't recall having had any great urge to get a higher education. I don't even remember consciously thinking the matter through."[1]

The ROTC

Powell lived at home with his parents and rode the bus to CCNY every day. At first, his major was engineering. But after one semester, Powell realized that field was not for him. He changed his major to geology, but Powell was not all that interested in that subject, either. But one aspect of CCNY did get his attention—the hundreds of students wearing military uniforms. When Powell returned for the fall semester, he found out they were part of the Reserve Officers' Training Corps (ROTC) program. They were training to be officers in the U.S. Army.

In the 1950s, CCNY had the largest ROTC program in the United States. As many as 1,500 men were enrolled in the program at one time. Powell did not hesitate to join. The first time he put on his uniform, he liked what he saw. "I felt somewhat

"Poor Man's Harvard"

City College of New York (CCNY) is located in Harlem. It was founded in 1847 as a college for children of immigrants, rich or poor. From the 1930s through the 1950s, its academics were so well regarded that it was proudly called the "Poor Man's Harvard."

distinctive wearing a uniform," Powell later said. "I hadn't been distinctive in much else."[2]

The military had only recently been desegregated, and many members still felt the effects of racism. However, Powell felt a sense of equality in his ROTC group. The cadets, as they were called, did everything together. They supported one another like brothers. Powell had never encountered anything like it before. He said of the experience, "I found a selflessness within our ranks that reminded me of the caring atmosphere within my family. Race, color, background, income meant nothing."[3]

One of the older cadets—Ronald Brooks— especially stood out. Powell was impressed by this tall, intelligent African-American cadet. Powell described him as sharp, quick, disciplined, and organized. Ronald Brooks became Powell's mentor and role model.

THE PERSHING RIFLES

Brooks was an officer in the Pershing Rifles, the most elite of the three ROTC drill teams. And that was the group Powell joined. He proudly wore the blue-and-white insignia and gold shoulder cords of the Pershing Rifles on his uniform.

The ROTC was just what Powell needed in his
life. He liked the discipline and structure of the
military. Tony Grant, one of Powell's neighbors in
the Bronx, said,

*He used to love pacing up and down the block, practicing
his marching, calling cadence out to himself, he thoroughly
enjoyed it. So it was
without question that
Colin was going to be
a [military] career
man.[4]*

NEW HOME

As Powell's
personal life was
improving, his
neighborhood
was deteriorating.
Rival gangs were
at war with each
other, brandishing
switchblades in
the streets. More
people were

The ROTC

The Reserve Officers' Training Corps (ROTC) officially began in 1916 when President Woodrow Wilson signed the National Defense Act. Military training had taken place in U.S. colleges and universities for nearly a century. The National Defense Act brought it under federal control.

The ROTC trains men and women on college campuses to become officers in the U.S. armed forces. Officers are trained in all branches except the U.S. Coast Guard. Students in the army and air force programs are referred to as cadets. In the navy, students are called midshipmen.

Upon completion of the program, students in the Army ROTC and Air Force ROTC are commissioned as second lieutenants. Students in the Navy ROTC join the navy and become ensigns or second lieutenants in the Marine Corps. Today, more than 20,000 college students are enrolled in ROTC army programs at more than 270 colleges and universities throughout the United States.

carrying guns. Many drug addicts also now lived in the neighborhood. Like so many other families, the Powells moved out of the Bronx.

More and more Bronx tenements sat empty, becoming prime targets for vandals and arsonists. The building at 952 Kelly Street, the Powells' home for 14 years, was eventually burned and torn down. Meanwhile, Luther Powell had figured out how to purchase a three-bedroom home for his family in the New York City borough of Queens. Colin now commuted to CCNY on the subway.

COMMANDER AND DRILLMASTER

In Powell's junior and senior years at college, the ROTC was his top priority. His hard work paid off. Powell became a cadet sergeant and then moved up to commander and drillmaster. The army was now paying him a monthly salary of $27.90.

Powell especially enjoyed the drill team competitions, which included both regular and trick categories. Powell led the 18-man trick drill team. They practiced drawing their M-I rifles, and they worked on diagonal marching, rifle spinning, and more. In spring of 1957, Powell's team won the trick competition, earning 492 points out of a possible 500. Perhaps Powell's surprise solo dance—the popular camel walk—had something to do with winning.

SECOND LIEUTENANT POWELL

On June 9, 1958, Powell was commissioned as a second lieutenant in the U.S. Army. With his fellow ROTC graduates, he repeated the army's oath:

I, Colin Luther Powell, do solemnly swear that I will support and defend the Constitution of the United States against all enemies foreign and domestic and that I will well and faithfully discharge the duties of the office upon which I am about to enter, so help me God.[5]

The oath sent a shiver down Powell's spine. The promise was one he would fulfill again and again in the course of his military career. Powell graduated from CCNY the next day. He received a bachelor's degree in geology.

Powell's first assignment was at Fort Benning, Georgia, in the heart

"Favorite Son"

In a 2001 interview with CNN, Colin Powell reflected on his college days. He noted that the City College of New York "let me in with my bad grades, and I stayed there for four and a half years, it was a four-year course, with bad grades. . . . And now I'm the favorite son, the most famous person who ever graduated from CCNY, and they give me all kinds of honors. And I smile, because they were sure anxious to see me go 35 years ago."[6]

of the South. Powell's commanding officer, Colonel Harold C. Brookhart, warned him about the South. He told Powell to be careful. The South was another world, nothing like New York. Powell would not fully understand what Brookhart meant until he arrived in Georgia.

Powell did not experience much racism at Fort Benning. But when he ventured to nearby Columbus, he was thrust into the raging prejudice of the South. He could shop at the local Woolworth's five-and-dime store, but he could not eat there. He was allowed to make purchases at a department store, but he was not allowed to use the men's room. Powell had rarely experienced prejudice; now he had no choice. But he faced it with dignity. "I did not feel inferior," he said, "and I was not going to let anybody make me believe I was. I was not going to allow someone else's feelings about me to become my feelings about myself."[7]

When Powell completed his training at Fort Benning, he escaped Southern racism and went to Gelnhausen, Germany, for two years. There, he could eat and shop wherever he wanted. For the first time, he was in command of a unit. It was 1958, and the cold war between the United States and the Soviet

Union was intensifying. Powell and his men readied for possible invasion and combat. The Soviet Union never attacked, but U.S. troops were prepared.

In 1961, Powell was assigned to Fort Devens, Massachusetts, near Boston. He was now a first lieutenant. That summer, he could have left the army. He had served the three years he had signed up for. But the army was all he knew, and he loved what he was doing.

A Blind Date

A couple months later, Powell discovered another love in his life. He met his future wife. In November 1961, Powell reluctantly went on a blind date. Alma Vivian Johnson was just as hesitant to go out with someone she had never met before. "I don't go out on blind dates," Alma told her roommate, "and I definitely don't go out with soldiers."[8]

Alma was from Birmingham, Alabama, and a graduate of Fisk University in Nashville, Tennessee.

A Segregated South

Colin Powell first experienced racial prejudice in 1958 when he was stationed in Georgia. Schools, restaurants, restrooms, drinking fountains, and more were legally segregated. Large signs told people what was "colored" and what was "white." From 1955 to 1968, African Americans such as Martin Luther King Jr., Rosa Parks, and Malcolm X tried to abolish racial discrimination. Lawsuits, boycotts, sit-ins, and freedom rides eventually led to several key pieces of legislation—the Civil Rights Act (1964), the Voting Rights Act (1965), and the Fair Housing Act (1968)—that enforced equal rights for African Americans.

She had come to Boston to further her education at Emerson College. Despite their doubts, Powell and Alma went on a blind date. They hit it off, and they soon fell in love.

In August 1962, Powell received new orders—he was going to South Vietnam. President John F. Kennedy had already sent 1,500 special advisers to this small southeastern Asian country that was being threatened by communism. Powell looked forward to his first assignment. But Alma was not happy. She was not interested in waiting a year to find out if their relationship would endure the separation. Two weeks later, on August 25, 1962, Colin and Alma were married in Birmingham. By the end of September, the couple was in Fort Bragg, North Carolina, where Colin took a Military Assistance Training Advisor course.

On December 23, Colin left his new bride and headed for the other side of the world. Alma, now pregnant, went home to Birmingham to live with her parents and wait for her husband to return. On Christmas morning, Colin Powell arrived in Saigon, South Vietnam.

Colin Powell and Alma Vivian Johnson were married on August 25, 1962.

U.S. troops aided the Army of the Republic of Vietnam during the Vietnam War.

Tour of Duty: Vietnam

On December 25, 1962, the weather was muggy and the colors vibrant in Saigon, South Vietnam. From the rooftop restaurant of his hotel, Captain Colin Powell observed Vietnamese culture for the first time. The streets of the busy capital were filled with pedicabs, bicycles, and small cars. Women in fashionable silk shopped from store to store. The people he observed were important to Powell—he hoped to save them from communism.

First Combat Assignment

A few days after Powell arrived, he headed north to the remote A Shau Valley along the mountainous border of Laos. This was his first combat assignment. Powell would spend most of his year trudging through the rugged, nearly uninhabited area. Captain Vo Cong Hieu was his Vietnamese counterpart. Hieu was an officer in the Army of the Republic of Vietnam (ARVN)—the noncommunist military forces of South Vietnam. Powell's job was to advise and train a 400-man Vietnamese battalion. Their job was to search for and fight the enemy—the National Liberation Front, which was popularly known as the Viet Cong.

Guerrilla Warfare

Outside the bustling city of Saigon, a crude, guerrilla war was going on. Fortresses of earth and wood lay hidden among the thick vegetation. Powell's quarters consisted of a thatched hut of bamboo and grass with a dirt floor and an occasional rat. The enemy was nearly invisible. The Viet Cong were experts at blending in with the dense layers of dangerous, dark jungle. Other times, they hid in a maze of underground tunnels that twisted and turned for more than 200 miles (322 km) beneath the small country.

Powell spent most of his time as a foot soldier. He tromped through dense jungles and swamps and scaled mountains. It was hot and muggy, but Powell wore a steel helmet, a long-sleeved green

Captain Vo Cong Hieu

In 1963, Colin Powell became good friends with his Vietnamese counterpart, Captain Vo Cong Hieu. Twenty-seven years later, Powell received a letter from Hieu. Enclosed was a 1963 photograph of the two friends. After spending 13 years in a communist re-education camp, Hieu had emigrated to the United States with his wife. He asked Powell to help get his married children and grandchildren out of Vietnam. Powell went to work. He contacted a friend who was able to get the rest of Hieu's family to the United States.

Two years later, Powell arrived for a speaking engagement at a Minnesota hotel. In the lobby stood his friend Vo Cong Hieu. Powell immediately embraced the small, poorly dressed man whose eyes were shimmering with tears. Powell insisted that Hieu join him for dinner and his speech. When Powell got up to speak, he began:

I ran into an old friend here, one I haven't seen for nearly thirty years. I want you to meet him, a new neighbor of yours and a new American, Vo Cong Hieu.[1]

Powell recalled that Hieu stood and looked surprised to be recognized. Powell was thankful for the opportunity he had to provide Hieu with freedom in the United States.

fatigue shirt, and long pants that tucked into his high-top boots. He had to protect himself against the razor-sharp elephant grass that could slice his skin. He also tried to avoid the leeches that would fall from the trees, attach themselves to his flesh, and suck out his blood. At all times, he was armed with a rifle. The enemy could be hiding anywhere, and Powell had to be ready.

What Is There to Eat?

On his first tour in Vietnam, Colin Powell ate what the Vietnamese ate: "Breakfast: rice stuck together with some glutinous substance and shaped into what looked like an edible softball. Lunch: rice with vegetables. Dinner: more rice, with chunks of pork or goat and, as an occasional treat, a two-inch-square omelet, actually quite tasty."[3]

The Viet Cong ambushed Powell's battalion almost every day, usually before sunrise. Still, Powell and the ARVN troops hardly ever saw their enemy. The Viet Cong acted quickly, killing a few of Powell's Vietnamese soldiers and then retreating. Powell's men returned fire, shooting into the jungle at an invisible enemy. "This was not war movies on a Saturday afternoon," Powell realized. "It was real, and it was ugly."[2]

THE BABY LETTER

Powell had little contact with his wife, Alma, while he was in Vietnam. Occasionally, he would receive a letter from her when an army helicopter dropped supplies and letters over the A Shau Valley. But sometimes letters took weeks or months to arrive. Powell knew he would soon be a father. He was eager to hear the news as soon as possible. He and Alma had worked out a plan. When she had the baby, she would write a letter and print the words "Baby Letter" on the envelope. Powell had told headquarters to watch for the letter, open it, and radio the news to him immediately.

On April 4, 1963, the supply helicopter dropped mail over Powell's camp. Powell received a letter from his mother that day. After filling him in on family news, she wrote, "Oh, by the way, . . . we are absolutely delighted about the baby."[4] What baby? Powell wondered. When he called headquarters, he found out that the envelope marked "Baby Letter" was sitting in a stack of undelivered mail. A radio operator then read Alma's important letter. Colin Powell's son—Michael Kevin—had been born on March 23, 1963. Powell was overjoyed. He also felt an increase in responsibility in his life. "A family back home was depending on me," he later wrote, "including a small new person. I wanted desperately to see this child. I had to make it through the year."[5]

Powell was injured by a punji spike.

Out of Action

The Viet Cong were armed with weapons
supplied by the Soviet Union and China. The
guerrillas also made their own primitive, but
dangerous, weapons. They used old tin cans and
wire to make booby traps and land mines. The
punji spike was one of their most dangerous
weapons. To make this deadly instrument, the Viet
Cong carved sharp points on the ends of wood or
bamboo sticks. They often contaminated the tips

The Tunnels

The Viet Cong guerrillas avoided open battles with U.S. troops. Instead, they carried out surprise ambushes and hit-and-run attacks. They were careful to hide their training bases and command headquarters from U.S. spotter planes. They built a vast system of underground tunnels equipped to provide everything the Viet Cong needed for weeks at a time. Tunnels housed arms factories, water supplies, weapons store rooms, kitchens, sleeping chambers, and hospitals.

of the sticks with feces to increase the victim's chance of infection. Then, hundreds of these spikes were stuck partially into the ground or in hidden pits camouflaged by brush or undergrowth.

In July 1963, while walking along a trail, Powell stepped into a hole concealed by jungle vegetation. In the hole were the dreaded punji spikes. One sharp bamboo stick pierced Powell's boot and came out the top of his instep. Powell finished up what he was doing before making the two-hour trek back to camp. By that time, he was in extreme pain from his badly swollen, purple, infected foot. A MEDVAC flew him to the nearest hospital for treatment. Powell received the Purple Heart for his injury. He was taken out of action and reassigned to headquarters in Hue, Vietnam.

"War" in Birmingham

Back in Alabama, where Alma and the baby lived, another kind of war was raging. It was a violent year in Birmingham, Alabama, and the rest of the South. In May, when Michael was only six weeks old, the police attacked a large group of antisegregation demonstrators. They turned dogs loose on the protesters and sprayed them with powerful fire hoses. On April 12, Martin Luther King Jr. was arrested in Birmingham for protesting without a permit. From jail, he wrote that disobeying the law was necessary if the laws were unfair. Titled *Letter from Birmingham Jail,* this piece would later be published as an article in the *Atlantic Monthly*.

The streets of Birmingham were not a safe place for African Americans. Many of them, including Alma and her family, stayed at home as much as possible. President Kennedy decided to help calm things down by sending National Guard troops to Birmingham.

The Fight for Civil Rights

On June 11, 1963, Kennedy addressed the nation on television. He declared, "The events in Birmingham and elsewhere have so increased the cries for equality that no city or State or legislative body can prudently choose to ignore them." He was going to ask Congress to "enact legislation giving all

Americans the right to be served in facilities which are open to the public—hotels, restaurants, theaters, retail stores, and similar establishments."[6]

On August 28, 1963, 250,000 people converged on Washington DC to support what would be called the Civil Rights Act. The voice of Martin Luther King Jr. resounded that day from the Lincoln Memorial as he delivered his famous "I have a dream" speech. Powell did not hear King's speech. In fact, he did not know what was going on in the United States. But Powell wanted this kind of equality for his new baby boy. He wanted it for Alma. He wanted it for himself. And he wanted it for everyone in the country.

Birmingham responded to Kennedy's speech with more violence. A Birmingham church was bombed, and four children were killed. A teenage boy was shot dead while riding a bicycle. Three months later, Powell returned to the United States. He found a different country from the one he had left a year before. ⁓

*Martin Luther King Jr. giving his "I have a dream" speech
at the Lincoln Memorial*

Segregation caused extreme social unrest in the southern United States.

A Master's and a Fellowship

On November 22, 1963, Colin Powell was in the Nashville, Tennessee, airport on his way home to Birmingham when he heard that President John F. Kennedy had been assassinated in Dallas, Texas. Vice President Lyndon B. Johnson

was immediately sworn in as the
new president of the United States.
President Johnson promised to carry
out Kennedy's plan to pass the Civil
Rights Act.

RACISM FIRSTHAND

Powell was reunited with his wife,
Alma. He also saw his eight-month-
old son, Michael, for the first time.
Powell was assigned to attend the
Infantry Officers Advanced Course
at Fort Benning, Georgia, in August.
Until then, Powell would do advanced
training for the U.S. Army Airborne
Rangers. Powell began looking for
housing for his family off of the base.
There were plenty of homes for white
officers. But Powell was restricted to
African-American neighborhoods.

Segregation was still strong in
the South. Few homes were available
for black families, and none were
suitable. Powell finally rented a house
that belonged to a Baptist minister

Assassins

On November 22, 1963, President John F. Kennedy was shot twice while riding in a motorcade in Dallas, Texas. The 46-year-old president was pronounced dead a half hour later. Less than two hours later, Lee Harvey Oswald was arrested at a nearby theater for assassinating the president. Oswald claimed he was innocent. Two days later, nightclub operator Jack Ruby gunned down and killed Oswald at police headquarters. Ruby was convicted and sentenced to death but won an appeal that granted him a new trial. Before the new trial date was set, Ruby died of cancer.

just across the border in Alabama. The home was decent, but it was located in the middle of a group of small, run-down houses. Powell also experienced racism firsthand in 1964. In Columbus, Georgia, he pulled his car into Buck's Barbecue drive-in and ordered a hamburger from his car. When the waitress saw his face, she told him he would have to go to the back door to be served. Powell sped off angrily without his hamburger.

Five months later, on July 2, 1964, President Johnson signed the Civil Rights Act into law. Businesses could no longer discriminate because of race. Powell went back to Buck's and ordered his hamburger. This time he was served, and he ate his food at the restaurant.

VIETNAM HEATS UP

In the fall of 1964, the war in Vietnam escalated. U.S. troops were no longer just advisers; they were engaged in all-out warfare. Powell, now a major, was stationed at Fort Leavenworth, Kansas, where he was taking an advanced officer training course. In February 1965, the army began air strikes against North Vietnam. Powell knew it was only a matter of time before he would be sent back into the war zone.

Meanwhile, Powell went about his duties and his training. He enjoyed the time he had with his growing family. On April 16, 1965, the Powells welcomed their second child, Linda Margaret, into the family. Powell was glad to be home for his daughter's birth. His duties and training at Leavenworth kept him in the United States and gave him the leadership training he would soon need.

In 1967 and 1968, Powell studied at the Army Command and General Staff College at Fort Leavenworth. He learned what he needed to train, supply, and transport an entire division of 10,000 troops. He learned how to manage them and make the best use of their skills in battle.

In 1968, the United States was in turmoil abroad and at home. At the beginning of the year, the communist guerrillas attacked

Fallen Comrades

Colin Powell lost many of his fellow soldiers in combat in Vietnam. Four of them had been his classmates at City College of New York. During the Vietnam War, more than 58,000 U.S. troops were killed. In 1982, each fallen soldier's name was engraved on the black granite slabs of the Vietnam Veterans Memorial in Washington DC.

more than 100 South Vietnamese cities, including Saigon, during the so-called Tet Offensive. They captured the U.S. embassy and attacked U.S. Army General William Westmoreland's headquarters. U.S. forces eventually took back the cities, but more troops were needed. President Johnson ordered 13,500 more soldiers to Vietnam. Meanwhile, the situation on the home front was grave. On April 4, 1968, Martin Luther King Jr. was assassinated in Memphis, Tennessee. Riots followed in major cities all across the United States.

Second Tour of Duty

In July 1968, Powell returned to Vietnam for his second tour of duty. He was temporary officer of operations and planning for 18,000 soldiers and 450 helicopters. He spent most of his time visiting army units throughout South Vietnam. In November, he boarded a helicopter called a Huey and headed to the jungle. Powell and seven others were celebrating the discovery of 29 Viet Cong camps and a weapons arsenal. The Huey, however, crashed as the pilot attempted to land. With a broken ankle, Powell heroically returned to the smoking aircraft and helped rescue four of his companions.

By the time Powell returned to Vietnam in July 1968,
the conflict had escalated.

BACK TO SCHOOL

On June 16, 1969, Powell received a letter from
George Washington University (GW) in Washington
DC. He had been accepted to the master's program
in the School of Government and Business
Administration. After finishing his tour in Vietnam
at the end of June, he started classes at GW that
fall. Colin and Alma bought a house and settled in
nearby Dale City, Virginia. The following year,

on May 20, the Powells had their
third child, Annemarie.

NATIONAL TURMOIL

Life was good for the Powells,
but the country was becoming more
chaotic. President Johnson had
announced early in 1968 that he
would not seek reelection. In 1969,
Richard Nixon became the thirty-
seventh president of the United
States. He had taken his oath of office
in January during the extreme unrest
of a divided America. War protesters
marched in the streets and shouted
antiwar slogans. Many Americans
openly, and sometimes violently,
condemned the Vietnam War.
College campuses often erupted in
violence over the conflict.

Over the next two years,
demonstrations, protests, bombings,
and contempt for the war intensified.
In April 1971, during Powell's final
semester at GW, Washington DC

The Powell Children

The Powell's oldest child, Michael Kevin Powell, was appointed by President Bill Clinton to the Federal Communications Commission (FCC) in 1997. In 2001, President George W. Bush named him chairman of the FCC. The Powells' daughter Linda became an actress, making her Broadway debut in 1993 in *Wilder, Wilder, Wilder*. Daughter Annemarie became a news producer for ABC's *Nightline*.

erupted. Hundreds of thousands of antiwar demonstrators swarmed the nation's capital to demand that the United States pull out of Vietnam. Members of a group called Vietnam Veterans Against the War threw more than 700 military medals on the steps of the Capitol building. Powell spoke out:

> *I understood their bitterness. . . . But my heart could never be with these demonstrators. I still believed in an America where medals ought to be a source of pride, not shame, where the uniform should be respected, not reviled, and where the armed forces were an honorable part of the nation, not a foreign body to be rejected by it.*[1]

Two weeks later, more than a thousand people were arrested for trying to shut down Congress. All together, more than 12,000 protesters were arrested in Washington DC that month.

In May, Powell graduated from GW with a master's of business administration. School had been different for Powell this time—he earned all As, except for one B. However, he did not attend his graduation. The antiwar atmosphere on campus was daunting, and he did not want to put his family in danger. Two months later, President Nixon began the long process of withdrawing U.S. troops from

Vietnam. It would be four years before the war was officially over.

In July 1971, Powell reported to the Pentagon, the headquarters of the U.S. Department of Defense. He was assigned to work in the office of Lieutenant General William E. DePuy, assistant vice chief of staff of the army. DePuy had a special assignment for Powell. He said, "Powell, I want you to take a couple of bright guys, go off into a corner, and start thinking the unthinkable."[2] He wanted Powell to help figure out how they would structure a drastically reduced

White House Fellows

President Lyndon B. Johnson established the White House Fellows program in 1964. He declared that "a genuinely free society cannot be a spectator society."[3] The purpose of the program is "to provide gifted and highly motivated young Americans with some first-hand experience in the process of governing the Nation and a sense of personal involvement in the leadership of society."[4] In return for their service, President Johnson hoped that White House fellows would become valuable contributors to and future leaders of the United States.

Applicants must be U.S. citizens who have completed their undergraduate education and are working in their chosen professions. A fellow normally works one year as a full-time assistant to top-ranking government officials such as the vice president, cabinet secretaries, and senior White House staff. The education portion of the program includes roundtable discussions with top leaders and trips to learn about U.S. domestic and foreign policy. The White House Fellowship has become one of the United States' most impressive leadership programs.

army once all the U.S. troops were home from Vietnam.

White House Fellow

In November 1971, an army major at the Pentagon handed Powell an eight-page application and told him to have it filled out by the weekend. It was an application for a White House Fellowship. Powell said he was not interested, but the major informed him that it was an order. Powell obeyed. Fellows were chosen each year to work in Washington DC and participate in the government process. Only people with extremely high potential were considered. Powell was one of 1,500 applicants. Only 17 would be chosen for the one-year appointment from 1972 to 1973.

Powell was selected for a White House Fellowship appointment that year. He served under President Nixon in the Office of Management and Budget. He worked closely with

Praise from Carlucci

Frank Carlucci, who would one day become secretary of defense, was impressed with Colin Powell. He reflected on Powell's work ethic when he was a White House fellow: "You gave him a project, it got done. It got done effectively. . . . It was easy to spot him as a rising talent at that time."[5]

Budget Director Caspar Weinberger and his top assistant, Frank Carlucci. One day, he would work with both of these men again—under very different circumstances. ⌣

Powell was a White House fellow in 1972.

Seoul, South Korea, in 1973

WHITE HOUSE GENERAL

olin Powell made a good impression during his one-year fellowship at the White House. He was asked to stay on in the Office of Management and Budget, but he turned down the offer. "The Army was my life," he later explained.[1]

SOUTH KOREA

Battalion commands were not easy to get. The waiting list was often long. But one command post—South Korea—was available, and Powell took it. Although Alma was not delighted with the idea of Colin being gone again, she supported her husband's decision. Their three children were ten, eight, and three years old.

In 1973, Powell arrived at Camp Casey in South Korea. Morale was at an all-time low. Many Americans had turned their backs on the military because of the Vietnam War. Soldiers were extremely demoralized. But Powell's leadership and optimism transformed these soldiers into disciplined, combat-ready troops. Powell recalled, "For me, this moment . . . with seven hundred once bedraggled soldiers now welded into a spirited whole, was magical, one of the treasured memories of my life."[2]

While Powell was in South Korea, the United States went through a stressful year. The Watergate scandal and likely impeachment of President Nixon forced the president to resign. When Powell returned in September 1974, Gerald Ford, once vice president under Nixon, was in the second month of his presidency.

BACK TO THE CLASSROOM

Powell was assigned temporarily to the Pentagon until August 1975. Then, he returned to the classroom. He had been selected to attend the National War College, a very prestigious institution in Washington DC. Approximately 140 students were accepted each year.

Halfway through the course, Powell was promoted to full colonel. Six weeks before he graduated, he overlapped school with a new military assignment. He would complete his academic work at Fort Campbell, Kentucky, while he commanded the 2nd Brigade of the 101st Airborne Division. This was the infamous Screaming Eagles division. General Dwight D. Eisenhower had led them to fame on D-Day, when the Allies invaded Normandy during World War II.

After seven years in the Washington DC area, Powell and

National War College

Established in 1946, the National War College prepares future leaders of all branches of the armed forces, the State Department, and civilian agencies. Courses include training for high-level responsibilities in national security. As of 2008, more than 7,500 students had graduated from the National War College.

The Powell family moved to Kentucky in 1975.

his family uprooted and moved to Kentucky. His
children liked being part of the Fort Campbell
community. Mike was comfortable being around
other military kids. After all, their fathers were all in
the same line of work. The children attended school
on the base. Annemarie, now six years old, was in
first grade. Eleven-year-old Linda supplemented
her education with music, especially the flute. And
Mike, now 13 years old, was catcher on the baseball

team. Alma was involved in volunteer work. She became somewhat of a mentor to the younger military wives.

Return to Washington

Powell was right where he wanted to be—commanding troops. But in 1977, he felt pressured to accept a Washington appointment. Jimmy Carter was now president, and Powell was offered two positions in his administration. Powell had no desire to take either one. But his commanding officer, Major General John Wickham, told him, "The Army is not going to pass up an opportunity to have one of its people in either of those key jobs."[3]

Stars

In the U.S. Army, the number of stars worn on generals' uniforms signifies their ranks. There are five levels for general, so they can receive up to five stars.

- General of the Army: five stars
- General: four stars
- Lieutenant General: three stars
- Major General: two stars
- Brigadier General: one star

In other words, Powell's appointment to either one of the positions would benefit the army. So, Powell accepted the position of executive assistant to John Kester, who was special assistant to the secretary and deputy secretary of defense. The Powells left Fort Campbell and moved back to the Washington DC area.

In December 1978, Powell was promoted to brigadier general. At 42, he was the youngest general in the U.S. Army. The promotion was a major step up for him. He celebrated with his family and friends. Aunts, uncles, cousins, friends, and ROTC buddies converged on Washington for the June 1, 1979, ceremony. Powell's mother came, but unfortunately, his father had died the year before. Powell wished his father could have seen him become a general. Powell joked, "Still, I felt that he was up there somewhere strutting among the other souls saying, 'Of course, what did you expect?'"[4] After the ceremony, approximately 150 people came to the Powells' home to celebrate.

Fast Track

Powell's career was now on the fast track. From 1979 to 1981 he served as senior military aide to

Maud Ariel "Arie" Powell

Colin Powell faced a personal crisis in June 1984 when his mother died. Both of his parents were now gone. "Parents are a luck of the draw," he said. "With my mother and father, I could not have been luckier."[5]

Deputy Secretary of Defense Graham Claytor. On their last day working together, Claytor predicted that Powell's career would continue to grow. Claytor said that he would not be surprised to see Powell as the chairman of the Joint Chiefs of Staff one day.

Powell spent the next two years commanding battalions at Fort Carson, Colorado, and Fort Leavenworth, Kansas. In 1983, he was promoted to major general, making him a two-star general. He also received a phone call from

Iran-Contra Affair

In the early 1980s, the United States agreed to sell weapons to Iran. In return, Iran would help secure the release of U.S. hostages from the terrorist Lebanese group Hezbollah. Iran was considered a supporter of the terrorists, so some of President Reagan's aides believed Iran could help free the hostages. Later, it was discovered that some of the profits from the weapons' sales were used to fund the Contras, an anticommunist rebel group in Nicaragua. A nationwide controversy developed.

Many saw the dealings as a dangerous break in U.S. policy, which was not to negotiate with terrorists. An investigation ensued. Reagan spoke to the public on March 4, 1987. He admitted that arms had been traded:

> What began as a strategic opening to Iran deteriorated . . . into trading arms for hostages. . . . There are reasons why it happened, but no excuses. It was a mistake.[6]

The investigation determined that Reagan did not know about the arms deal. However, 11 of his officials were convicted, including Oliver North, John Poindexter, and Secretary of Defense Caspar Weinberger. In 1992, at the end of the George H. W. Bush administration, the convictions of North and Poindexter were overturned on appeal and Weinberger was pardoned prior to his trial.

Caspar Weinberger, his old friend and supervisor from his year as a White House fellow. Weinberger was now secretary of defense in President Ronald Reagan's administration. He asked Powell to be his military assistant. Reluctantly, Powell accepted the position and once again returned to Washington. Powell worked for Weinberger for nearly three years. Together, they dealt with the U.S. invasion of Grenada, the Iran-Contra Affair, which sparked controversy about the U.S. negotiating with terrorists in the early 1980s, and more. Powell walked away from the position with much praise for the man he called a great fighter and a brilliant advocate.

In 1986, Powell was once again commanding troops—75,000 in Frankfurt, West Germany. This time, Powell's wife and children went with him. Powell also had the privilege of commanding his own son, who was

**Second Lieutenant
Michael Powell**

In May 1985, Powell spoke at the ROTC commissioning ceremony at the College of William and Mary in Virginia. Twenty-seven years had passed since he had received his own commission. Now, he had the privilege of commissioning, or awarding rank to, his son, Michael. As the cadets crossed the stage, Powell embraced his son. Military leadership had come full circle for father and son. However, in 1987, Michael was severely injured in a jeep accident while stationed in West Germany. He was hospitalized for a year of painful rehabilitation. The accident ended his military career.

stationed there. That year, Powell was promoted to lieutenant general. He was now a three-star general.

In November, he received another call from an old friend—Frank Carlucci—who had just been named national security advisor. Carlucci asked Powell to be his deputy. In fact, he begged him to come back to Washington. The Iran-Contra Affair was still a mess, and the presidency itself was at stake. Powell turned down Carlucci's offer, but a phone call from the president changed Powell's mind. ⌐

Caspar Weinberger

*Powell and Alma during Powell's farewell ceremony in Germany
before their return to the United States*

Up the Political Ladder

On December 12, 1986, President
Ronald Reagan phoned Colin Powell
in Germany. Reagan needed help with the Iran-
Contra Affair. He asked Lieutenant General Powell
to return to Washington. Powell accepted without

hesitation. Though he had turned down Carlucci, he could not say no to the president of the United States.

Powell worked with Carlucci to deal with the Iran-Contra Affair and to restore the reputation of the National Security Council, which had helped carry out the controversial Iran-Contra operations. The following year, Carlucci became secretary of defense. Powell also moved up the political ladder. He became deputy assistant to the president for national security affairs. He was the first black American to hold that position.

It was an interesting time to be in the president's inner circle. Reagan was upping the stakes in the cold war. He was developing a nuclear defense system called the Strategic Defense Initiative that would protect the United States from a nuclear attack by the Soviet Union. However, this defense system never made much progress. Reagan also labeled the Soviet Union an "evil empire." He challenged Soviet President Mikhail Gorbachev to tear down the Berlin Wall, a symbol of Soviet power that was separating communist East Germany from West Germany. And Reagan asked for Soviet arms reduction. It was Powell's job to negotiate directly with Soviet leaders

"Look for intelligence and judgment and, most critically, a capacity to anticipate, to see around corners. Also look for loyalty, integrity, a high energy drive, a balanced ego and the drive to get things done."[1]

—Colin Powell, explaining what he looks for in a coworker

to reduce their long-range nuclear missiles.

On November 8, 1988, George H. W. Bush was elected president. He had served as Reagan's vice president for the past eight years. Bush knew what Powell had accomplished for Reagan and wanted him on his team. On November 9, Bush offered Powell several choices: he could serve as deputy secretary of state, as head of the Central Intelligence Agency (CIA), or stay on as national security advisor.

The army also wanted Powell. They offered him a position that would make him a four-star general, the army's highest rank. He would be commander in chief of Forces Command (FORSCOM), in charge of nearly 1 million troops. In a few days, Powell told President-elect Bush that he was returning to the army. Bush accepted his answer graciously.

CHAIRMAN OF THE JOINT CHIEFS OF STAFF

In January 1989, after Bush's inauguration, Powell left for Fort McPherson, Georgia. But his time there was short. In August, President Bush

President George H. W. Bush, left, named Powell chairman
of the Joint Chiefs of Staff during a ceremony in 1989.

and Secretary of Defense Dick Cheney asked Powell
to become chairman of the Joint Chiefs of Staff.
This position would make him the highest-ranking
military officer in the U.S. armed forces and the
main military adviser to the National Security
Council, the secretary of defense, and the president.
Powell accepted. He was the first black American and
the first ROTC graduate to receive the appointment.
At 52, he was also the youngest appointee.

Powell began his new job on October 1. In the middle of his first night on the job, he received a phone call. An uprising was brewing in Panama. Members of the Panamanian military were planning to overthrow the government led by dictator Manuel Noriega. The coup took place two days later.

Panama had been a hot spot since the Reagan years. Now, pressure mounted for Bush to help the people of Panama. Powell advised Bush to use military force to remove Noriega from power. Bush agreed, and Powell planned an invasion. Operation Just Cause, as it was called, began on December 20, 1989. Noriega surrendered to the U.S. military on January 3, 1990. In Panama, people danced in the streets.

OPERATION DESERT STORM

Less than a year later, Powell was handling another conflict on the other side of the world. On the evening of August 1, 1990, Powell's secure phone rang. Saddam Hussein had just sent his Iraqi army across the border and into Kuwait. Hussein claimed that Kuwait belonged to Iraq. Warning signs earlier in the summer had indicated that Iraq might invade this small, oil-rich country. Powell had been working with General Norman Schwarzkopf to come up with a plan if Iraq invaded Kuwait. Now, Powell put his leadership and strategic skills into high gear.

Within hours, the United States requested a meeting with the United Nations (UN). On August 2, the UN passed a resolution condemning the invasion and demanded withdrawal of Iraqi troops. By August 6, the UN had placed economic sanctions on Iraq—countries could not buy from or sell to Iraq, crippling the nation's economy. The next day, U.S. troops were deployed to nearby Saudi Arabia. U.S. battleships positioned themselves in the area. The United States also urged other countries to send forces to the Middle East. Thirty-four countries offered their support.

Iraq was given a deadline of January 15, 1991, to withdraw from Kuwait. On January 16, Iraqi

General Norman H. Schwarzkopf Jr.

General Norman H. Schwarzkopf Jr. was commander of the Coalition Forces in the 1991 Persian Gulf War. In just a few months, he rallied 765,000 troops from 28 countries. He also brought together thousands of planes and tanks and hundreds of battleships. He was given much of the credit for ending the ground war in four days. Earlier in his career, he had served two tours of duty in Vietnam, where he earned the reputation of being an officer who would risk his life for other soldiers.

forces were still there; the United States launched Operation Desert Storm. It began with a massive aerial bombing campaign in Iraq. Initially, Powell was hesitant to take military action. But a week later, at a televised Pentagon news conference, Powell told the nation: "Our strategy for going after this army is very, very simple. First we are going to cut it off, and then we are going to kill it."[2]

On February 24, 1991, U.S. ground troops swept through Kuwait, pushed out the Iraqis, and crossed the border into Iraq. Bush

The Powell Doctrine

After the Persian Gulf War in 1991, Colin Powell outlined his view of effective military action in an article in the winter 1992 edition of *Foreign Affairs* magazine. Powell called it a "when-to-go-to-war doctrine." He posed questions that leaders should ask before going to war:

- *Is the political objective we seek to achieve important, clearly defined and understood?*
- *Have all other nonviolent policy means failed?*
- *Will military force achieve the objective?*
- *At what cost?*
- *Have the gains and risks been analyzed?*
- *How might the situation that we seek to alter, once it is altered by force, develop further and what might be the consequences?*[3]

Powell concluded,

In those circumstances where we must use military force, we have to be ready, willing and able. Where we should not use force we have to be wise enough to exercise restraint.[4]

called for a cease-fire at midnight on February 27 and declared Kuwait liberated. On April 6, Iraq accepted the United Nations' terms.

This short-lived Persian Gulf War, as it was called, was over. Fewer than 150 U.S. soldiers were killed in battle. Iraq's military was crippled. But the war had stopped short of capturing Saddam Hussein and removing him from power. The following year, Powell shrugged off Hussein. He explained:

> *Even if we had been able to capture him, what purpose would it have served? And would serving that purpose have been worth the many more casualties that would have occurred? Would it have been worth the inevitable follow-up: major occupation forces in Iraq for years to come . . . ? Fortunately for America, reasonable people at the time thought not.[5]*

Kuwaiti Oil Fires

When Iraqi troops were forced out of Kuwait in February 1991, they set fire to Kuwaiti oil fields as they retreated. The fires burned for months. Approximately 6 million barrels of oil burned up each day. Before the fires could be extinguished, the military had to remove land mines that the Iraqis had placed around the oil wells. All the fires were eventually put out by private companies. Having the fires extinguished cost Kuwait approximately $1.5 billion.

Twelve years later, Powell would again have to deal with Iraq and Saddam Hussein. In the Iraq War, as it would be called, Hussein would be captured and eventually tried and hanged. But the war would be controversial, and public opinion would be divided.

Powell met with troops in Saudi Arabia.

Powell did not always agree with President Clinton's policies.

CIVILIAN LIFE

*I*n the aftermath of the Persian Gulf War, Colin Powell became a national hero. Americans were proud of their military. The swift victory and the liberation of Kuwait had been impressive. People recognized Powell's strong leadership skills. His popularity soared. Many Americans hoped he would run for president, or at least vice president, of the United States.

Next Vice President?

It was an election year in 1992. President Bush, who was running for a second term, was being pressured to drop Dan Quayle as his vice-presidential running mate. The press repeatedly mentioned Powell as a likely replacement. Polls showed that people favored Powell on the Republican ticket. But Powell had no intention of accepting such a nomination. In the middle of May, Powell made a phone call to Dan Quayle assuring him that he was not the source of the speculation and that he intended to keep his job as chairman of the Joint Chiefs of Staff.

That same month, Vernon Jordan from the Bill Clinton campaign contacted Powell. Arkansas Governor Clinton was probably going to win the Democratic nomination. Jordan asked Powell if he was interested in running as vice president with Clinton. Powell responded, "I don't intend to step out of uniform one day and into partisan politics the next."[1] Powell would not run on either ticket.

HOMOSEXUALITY AND THE MILITARY

In November 1992, Bill Clinton won the presidential election. Powell stayed on as chairman of the Joint Chiefs of Staff through August 1993. Powell and Clinton did not see eye-to-eye on a number of issues. One topic that they disagreed on was homosexuals in the military. During his campaign, Clinton had promised to end the ban on homosexuals serving in the armed forces. Now, the president intended to fulfill his promise. Powell did not agree. The topic became heated throughout the nation. Many people supported Powell's desire to keep the ban. But others strongly disagreed, and Powell became a target of media and public criticism. Powell and Clinton eventually came to a compromise. It was called the "don't ask, don't tell" policy—homosexuals could serve as long as they kept their sexual orientation a secret.

Anyone for a Volvo?

Colin Powell likes cars. He especially enjoys fixing up old Volvos. At Powell's retirement celebration in 1993, President Bill Clinton presented him with a rusted-out 1966 Volvo. Working on old Volvos was a way for Powell to relax on weekends. Once he fixed them up, he would drive around in them.

RETIREMENT

At the end of September 1993, Powell retired from the military after 35 years of service. He left the career he most loved. The four-star general was now a civilian. Powell's farewell ceremony was spectacular. His family came to celebrate, as did comrades from the ROTC and friends from five presidential administrations. The drum and bugle corps performed, cannons fired a 19-gun salute, and the army band played "Eye of the Storm: The General Colin L. Powell March." Then, President Clinton presented Powell with the Presidential Medal of Freedom with Distinction. Powell had already received one Presidential Medal of Freedom from President George H. W. Bush after the Persian Gulf War. Now, he had two. Powell later recalled his final day with the army:

> *That night, I took off the uniform for the last time. In the years I had worn it, I had benefited beyond my wildest hopes from all that is good in this country, and I had*

Presidential Medal of Freedom

The Presidential Medal of Freedom is the United States' highest nonmilitary award. Established in 1945 by President Harry Truman, the award initially recognized exceptional service in World War II. In 1963, President John F. Kennedy changed the focus of the award to distinguished civilian service in peacetime. Approximately 400 medals have been awarded since its inception.

Powell and Alma at his retirement ceremony

overcome its lingering faults. I had found something to do with my life that was honorable and useful, that I could do well, and that I loved doing. That is rare good fortune in anyone's life. My only regret was that I could not do it all over again.[2]

Focus on U.S. Youth

Powell now turned his focus to America's youth, especially those in the inner city. His first step was to increase the number of Junior ROTC (JROTC) programs in the nation's high schools. He believed teenagers would benefit from the discipline, work ethic, and pride of membership in the JROTC. He also believed society would greatly benefit from more kids with purpose and high self-esteem.

Powell began his mission in New York City. No public high school offered JROTC there, and only one private school had the program. Before long, JROTC was in seven high schools, including Morris High School, where Powell had attended.

Four years later, Powell would attend the President's Summit for America's Future in Philadelphia. Also present would be 4 presidents, 30 governors, 100 mayors, and

Knighted

On December 15, 1993, Colin and Alma Powell were guests at Buckingham Palace, the home of England's Queen Elizabeth II. The queen conferred on Powell the title of honorary knight commander of the Order of the Bath, a British order of chivalry.

many community leaders. They would challenge the United States to make children and youth a national priority. Out of the summit would grow America's Promise Alliance. Powell, the founding chairman, would put his enthusiasm for helping youth into action. He believed that when too many children are at risk, the United States is a nation at risk. The organization would commit to helping children receive the fundamental resources they need to succeed. Called the Five Promises, they are caring adults, safe places,

America's Promise Alliance

Colin Powell founded America's Promise Alliance in 1997. The organization works to put young people on a path toward successful adulthood. It partners with more than 100 corporations, nonprofit organizations, foundations, policy makers, advocacy organizations, and faith-based groups to ensure that America's youth receive the Five Promises—caring adults, safe places, a healthy start, effective education, and opportunities to help others.

In 2007, the goal of America's Promise Alliance became "15 in 5"—improving the lives of 15 million at-risk young people over five years. The top priority is to reduce high-school dropout rates. Other services provided include making sure youth have health insurance and informing young people about community services. It also gives middle-school students the chance to experience community service and career exploration by creating real-world opportunities.

When Hurricane Katrina hit the Gulf Coast in 2005, America's Promise Alliance formed Katrina's Kids. Its goal is to help young people displaced by natural disasters receive the resources they need. As of 2009, the organization continued to work with officials in Louisiana, Mississippi, and Texas to make communities even stronger than they were before Katrina.

a healthy start, effective education, and opportunities to help others.

HAITI DELEGATION

Powell was enjoying civilian life. Volunteering and spending time with his family filled his time with meaningful activities. But Powell's military skills would still prove valuable to the United States. A year after Powell's retirement, President Clinton asked for his help to prevent a U.S. invasion of Haiti, a country in the West Indies. Powell went to Haiti with former President Jimmy Carter and Senator Sam Nunn of Georgia on September 17, 1994. Theirs was a last-minute effort to convince Haiti's dictator and ruling military leaders to step down. After more than 24 hours of negotiation, the Carter-Powell-Nunn delegation was successful. Haiti returned to a government run by its elected leaders.

My American Journey

After Colin Powell's retirement from the military, he began writing his autobiography, *My American Journey*. Published in 1995, the book received rave reviews and much public attention. By the end of its first week of sales, the book hit the *New York Times* best-seller list. At his first author event, Powell signed more than 3,000 books in just a few hours. Massive crowds wanted his autograph, but they also wanted to convince him to run for president of the United States. Powell thought about running for president but decided against it.

In December 1994, Clinton asked Powell to be his secretary of state. Powell politely declined. However, seven years later, Powell would find himself serving in that position under another president, George W. Bush. ⌐

*Powell, left, Sam Nunn, center, and Jimmy Carter, right,
returning from Haiti negotiations*

From left to right, *Secretary of State Powell, President Bush, and Vice President Cheney during a meeting after the September 11 attacks*

Secretary of State

G eorge W. Bush took office as president of the United States in January 2001. Colin Powell had served under Bush's father as chairman of the Joint Chiefs of Staff. Now, the younger Bush asked Powell to be secretary of state. Powell accepted.

He was approved unanimously by the U.S. Senate. It was the highest office at that time ever to be held by a black American.

PUT TO THE TEST

As secretary of state, Powell was the president's highest-ranking cabinet member. His primary duty was to advise the president on foreign affairs. On September 11, 2001, less than eight months after Bush took office, the United States was attacked. Al-Qaeda, an international terrorist organization led by Osama bin Laden, took credit for the attack. Powell was in Peru when the terrorists crashed commercial airplanes into the World Trade Center and the Pentagon and caused another to go down in Shanksville, Pennsylvania. He immediately headed back to the United States. On board his plane, Powell told the press:

> [T]he United States Government will do everything to find the perpetrators of this cowardly attack against innocent people and bring them to justice. . . . Let there be no doubt that buildings can be destroyed and precious lives can be

Who Is Responsible?

After the September 11, 2001, terrorist attacks on the United States, Powell stated publicly, "We will find out who is responsible for this and they will pay for it. This has got to be a full-scale assault by the civilized community against terrorism."[1]

lost but our society cannot be destroyed and our democracy cannot be destroyed. Our spirit as a nation cannot be destroyed. [2]

For the rest of Powell's term, his foreign affairs skills were put to the test. He worked with world leaders to plan and carry out an attack against al-Qaeda and fight the war on terrorism. The first target was Afghanistan, which funded and protected al-Qaeda. The invasion of Afghanistan was called Operation Enduring Freedom. Powell was praised for his part in overthrowing Afghanistan's

The Taliban

The United States' target in Afghanistan after the September 11, 2001, attacks was the Taliban. The Taliban, a religious and political movement, had come into power after ending the nonstop fighting among warlords in Afghanistan in 1994. At first, Afghans welcomed the Taliban and the order it restored to their country. But then the Taliban's extremely strict regulations led to human rights violations, especially for women. Education for girls was banned, and women were not allowed to work. They were beaten publicly and executed for disobeying their husbands or Taliban laws.

After al-Qaeda attacked the United States in 2001, the U.S. government made demands of the Taliban. The Afghani group had to turn over Osama bin Laden and other leaders of al-Qaeda to the United States and allow access to terrorist training camps. The Taliban refused.

On October 7, 2001, the United States and other countries bombed Taliban and al-Qaeda camps and entered Afghanistan. They removed the Taliban from power. Five years later, in 2006, the Taliban made a comeback and attempted to regain control of Afghanistan. As of 2009, the conflict continued.

Taliban regime and hunting down many suspected terrorists.

Addressing the United Nations

In 2002, the Bush administration focused on Iraq. The renewed interest in this Middle Eastern country took Powell back more than a decade to the Persian Gulf War. The United States was pursuing an old enemy, Saddam Hussein. CIA intelligence suggested that Hussein's regime was producing weapons of mass destruction (WMDs)—nuclear, chemical, and biological weapons. Hussein had used chemical weapons in the past. In 1988, he dropped nerve gas and mustard gas on his own people. The United Nations had ordered Iraq to destroy the WMDs. Some intelligence sources warned the Bush administration that Hussein was indeed stockpiling these weapons. They also suggested that Hussein was aiding al-Qaeda. Other intelligence sources did not think that Hussein had WMDs and they informed the Bush administration of their doubts.

Powell encouraged diplomacy in dealing with Iraq. He wanted the president to work with the United Nations. On February 5, 2003, however,

Powell addressed the United Nations Security Council on February 5, 2003.

Powell made a surprising 90-minute speech to the United Nations Security Council:

> *There can be no doubt that Saddam Hussein has biological weapons and the capability to rapidly produce more, many more. And he has the ability to dispense these lethal poisons and diseases in ways that can cause massive death and destruction.*[3]

He outlined the evidence against
Iraq and made the case for war.
He concluded, "Leaving Saddam
Hussein in possession of weapons
of mass destruction for a few more
months or years is not an option, not
in a post-September 11th world."[4]

ATTACK ON IRAQ

The United Nations did not
agree. However, in March 2003,
the United States, Great Britain,
and other allies invaded Iraq in what
would be called the Iraq War despite
great opposition from the rest of the
world. The Iraqi regime was toppled,
but Saddam Hussein avoided capture
for more than eight months. In
December 2003, U.S. troops caught
Hussein. He was later tried and
hanged. Most of the world approved
that such a cruel dictator was gone.
However, after a year of searching
for WMDs, none were uncovered.
Powell, Bush, and other members

**United Nations
Security Council**

The purpose of the
United Nations Security
Council is to maintain
international peace and
security. When the coun-
cil receives word of a
threat to peace, it usually
recommends first that the
parties try to agree peace-
fully. It also may submit
principles for a peaceful
settlement. When a settlement cannot be reached,
the council sometimes
enforces economic sanc-
tions or military action.

of the administration came under harsh criticism. Some people pointed to evidence that, prior to the invasion, the Bush administration had pushed intelligence agencies to falsely state that Iraq had WMDs and ties to al-Qaeda.

On November 15, 2004, Powell resigned as secretary of state. Although Powell stated that his move was voluntary, he made it clear that he had been forced out of his position. His friends claimed that Powell disagreed with the Bush administration on many issues, making his work too difficult. Powell had been worried to go forward with the Iraq War without the support of the United Nations. Later, he expressed regret over the war. In a September 2005 interview with Barbara Walters, Powell reflected on his call for war in his speech at the United Nations. He called it a "blot" on his record.

> *I'm the one who presented it to the world, and [it] will always be a part of my record. It was painful. It is painful now. . . . The intelligence system did not work well.*[5]

RETURN TO PRIVATE LIFE

Powell was again a private citizen. He filled his time with a variety of activities and ventures. He invested in an Internet company, attempted to buy a new baseball franchise, and became a partner in a technology firm. His public speaking engagements filled up his calendar. He especially enjoyed speaking at schools and youth centers. His passion was still alive to help the nation's disadvantaged young people, and he continued to strongly support America's Promise Alliance. In 2008 and 2009, Powell served as spokesperson for National Mentoring Month, an annual event to recruit mentors for at-risk youth.

Powell kept a low profile after he stepped out of politics in 2004. However, in October 2008, he briefly came back into the political world. Just two weeks before the presidential election, Powell announced his support for Barack Obama, the Democratic candidate.

No one knows what the future may hold for Colin Powell. But

Independent, Republican, or Democrat?

Although Colin Powell served mostly under Republican presidents, he was registered as a member of the Independent Party. In 1995, he became a Republican and actively campaigned for Republican presidential candidate Bob Dole. In the 2008 presidential race, Powell supported Republican candidate John McCain. However, just two weeks before the presidential election, Powell announced that he would be voting for Democratic nominee Barack Obama.

this former national security advisor, chairman of the Joint Chiefs of Staff, and secretary of state has enjoyed a lifetime of accomplishments. He achieved the highest rank in the U.S. Army and served in the administrations of six U.S. presidents. Most of all, he captured the hearts and the respect of the American people. But to Powell, only one thing is important—that he be remembered as "a good public servant. Somebody who truly believed in his country, loved it and served to the best of his ability." Powell humbly said, "As long as I'm remembered as somebody who served, that's good enough for me."[6]

Colin Powell

TIMELINE

1937	1954	1958
Colin Powell is born April 5 in Harlem.	Powell begins attending City College of New York, where he joins the ROTC and commands the Pershing Rifles drill team.	Powell graduates from college and is commissioned as second lieutenant in the U.S. Army.

1967–1968	1968	1968
Powell studies at the Army Command and General Staff College at Fort Leavenworth, Kansas.	Powell arrives in Vietnam on July 27 for his second tour of duty.	In November, Powell is injured during a helicopter crash.

1962	1962	1963
Powell marries Alma Vivian Johnson on August 25.	Powell is deployed to South Vietnam on December 23.	Powell is injured by a punji spike in July.

1971	1972–1973	1975
Powell earns a master's of business administration degree from George Washington University in May.	Powell serves as a White House fellow.	Powell attends National War College. He is promoted to colonel.

TIMELINE

1977	1979–1981	1983
Powell serves in the Carter administration under the special assistant to the secretary and deputy secretary of defense.	Powell serves as senior military aide to the deputy secretary of defense.	Powell is promoted to major general. He becomes military assistant to Secretary of Defense Caspar Weinberger.

1989	1993	1994
Powell serves as chairman of the Joint Chiefs of Staff in the George H. W. Bush and Bill Clinton administrations.	Powell retires as chairman of the Joint Chiefs of Staff. He also retires from the military after 35 years of service.	Powell joins former President Carter and Senator Sam Nunn on a last-minute peacemaking trip to Haiti.

1986 1987 1988

1986 Powell is promoted to lieutenant general and serves as deputy to National Security Advisor Frank Carlucci.

1987 Powell serves in the Reagan administration as assistant to the president for national security affairs.

1988 Powell becomes a four-star general and commander in chief of Forces Command.

1997 2001 2004

1997 Powell founds America's Promise Alliance to help at-risk youth.

2001 President George W. Bush appoints Powell secretary of state. Powell takes a leading role in the war on terrorism.

2004 Powell resigns as secretary of state on November 15.

ESSENTIAL FACTS

DATE OF BIRTH

April 5, 1937

PLACE OF BIRTH

Harlem, New York City

PARENTS

Luther Theophilus Powell and Maud Ariel "Arie" McKoy Powell

EDUCATION

Morris High School; City College of New York; Army Command and General Staff College; George Washington University; National War College

MARRIAGE

Alma Vivian Johnson (August 25, 1962)

CHILDREN

Michael Kevin (1963), Linda Margaret (1965), Annemarie (1970)

CAREER HIGHLIGHTS

Joining the Reserve Officers' Training Corps in college gave Powell's life direction and boosted his self-esteem. During Powell's two tours of duty in the Vietnam War, he was awarded the Purple Heart, the Bronze Star, and the Soldier's Medal. In 1972, Powell began serving one year in Washington DC as a White House fellow.

Powell became a four-star general at the age of 51 and became commander in chief of Forces Command. Starting in 1989, Powell served as chairman of the Joint Chiefs of Staff under President George H. W. Bush and President Bill Clinton. In 2001, Powell was appointed secretary of state for the first term of the George W. Bush administration.

SOCIETAL CONTRIBUTION

Colin Powell is the founding chairman of America's Promise Alliance, a nonprofit organization committed to helping at-risk youth.

CONFLICTS

Colin Powell faced racism and discrimination throughout his life. As a child, Powell struggled with academics and sports in school. Later, Powell received several injuries during the Vietnam War. In the early 1990s, Powell and President Bill Clinton conflicted over whether to allow homosexuals in the military. In 2003, the United Nations disagreed with Powell's rationale for the Iraq War.

QUOTE

"I had found something to do with my life that was honorable and useful, that I could do well, and that I loved doing. That is rare good fortune in anyone's life. My only regret was that I could not do it all over again."—*Colin Powell*

ADDITIONAL RESOURCES

SELECT BIBLIOGRAPHY

Astor, Gerald. *The Right to Fight: A History of African Americans in the Military*. Cambridge, MA: Da Capo, 2001.

Brokaw, Tom. *Boom! Voices of the Sixties: Personal Reflections on the '60s and Today*. New York, NY: Random House, 2007.

DeYoung, Karen. *Soldier: The Life of Colin Powell*. New York, NY: Alfred A. Knopf, 2006.

Means, Howard. *Colin Powell: A Biography*. New York, NY: Ballantine Books, 1992.

Powell, Colin L. *My American Journey*. New York, NY: Random House, 1995.

FURTHER READING

Brown, Warren. *Colin Powell: Soldier and Statesman*. New York, NY: Chelsea House Publishers, 2005.

Englar, Mary. *Colin Powell*. Chicago, IL: Raintree, 2006.

Horn, Geoffrey M. *Colin Powell*. Milwaukee, WI: World Almanac Library, 2005.

Wheeler, Jill C. *Colin Powell*. Edina, MN: Abdo & Daughters, 2002.

WEB LINKS

To learn more about Colin Powell visit ABDO Publishing Company online at **www.abdopublishing.com**. Web sites about Colin Powell are featured on our Book Links page. These links are routinely monitored and updated to provide the most current information available.

Places to Visit

The Pentagon
1400 Defense Pentagon, Washington, DC 20301-1400
703-697-1776
pentagon.afis.osd.mil
Tours educate about missions of the U.S. Department of Defense and each of its branches of service. They also highlight significant moments in military history.

The Vietnam Veterans Memorial
National Park Service, National Capitol Parks-Central
900 Ohio Drive Southwest, Washington, DC 20242
202-426-6841 or 202-619-7225
thewall-usa.com
See the wall that memorializes the names of those who died in the Vietnam War or are still missing.

The White House
1600 Pennsylvania Avenue Northwest, Washington, DC 20500
202-456-2121
www.whitehouse.gov
Tours are available to view the building where the president lives and works.

GLOSSARY

battalion
Army unit consisting of a headquarters and two or more companies.

borough
One of the five self-governing units of New York City.

cache
A hidden store of weapons.

cadet
A student in training to be an officer in the military.

commission
To authorize for active military service.

communism
A political system in which the government controls the economy and property is shared and owned by the community.

coup
A sudden and decisive change of government that happens illegally or by force.

emigrate
To leave one's native country or region to settle in another.

guerrilla
A member of a group of fighters who attack suddenly and fight by sabotage and harassment.

infantry
Soldiers trained to fight on foot.

intelligence
Secret information about an enemy, used especially for military purposes.

negotiation
>The process of discussing in order to reach an agreement.

pedicab
>A small three-wheeled vehicle with a seat, pedals, and handlebars for the operator and usually a covered cab in back for passengers.

piecework
>Work paid for according to the number of units turned out.

prejudice
>Irrational suspicion or hatred of a particular group, race, or religion.

Purple Heart
>U.S. military award given to members of the armed forces who have been wounded in action.

racism
>The belief that race accounts for differences in human character or ability; belief that a particular race is superior to others.

ROTC
>Reserve Officers' Training Corps; a training program that prepares college students to be commissioned officers.

tenement
>A run-down, low-rent apartment building.

Source Notes

Chapter 1. Huey Down

1. Colin Powell and Joseph E. Persico. *My American Journey*. New York: Random House, 1995. 138.

Chapter 2. Growing Up in New York

1. Colin Powell and Joseph E. Persico. *My American Journey*. New York: Random House, 1995. 60.

2. Eric Foner, John Arthur Garraty, and Society of American Historians. *The Reader's Companion to American History*. Boston: Houghton Mifflin, 1991. 487.

3. Colin Powell and Joseph E. Persico. *My American Journey*. New York: Random House, 1995. 11.

4. Ibid. 19.

Chapter 3. An Army Career

1. Howard Means. *Colin Powell: A Biography*. New York: Ballantine Books, 1992. 68.

2. "Encore Presentation: Colin Powell: From Military Leader to Career Diplomat." *People in the News*. CNN.com. 6 Jan. 2001. 6 Apr. 2009 <http://transcripts.cnn.com/TRANSCRIPTS/0101/06/ pitn.00.html>.

3. Gerald Astor. *The Right to Fight: A History of African Americans in the Military*. Cambridge, MA: Da Capo, 2001. 414.

4. "Encore Presentation: Colin Powell: From Military Leader to Career Diplomat." *People in the News*. CNN.com. 6 Jan. 2001. 6 Apr. 2009 <http://transcripts.cnn.com/TRANSCRIPTS/0101/06/ pitn.00.html>.

5. Colin Powell and Joseph E. Persico. *My American Journey*. New York: Random House, 1995. 36.

6. "Encore Presentation: Colin Powell: From Military Leader to Career Diplomat." *People in the News*. CNN.com. 6 Jan. 2001. 6 Apr. 2009 <http://transcripts.cnn.com/TRANSCRIPTS/0101/06/ pitn.00.html>.

7. Colin Powell and Joseph E. Persico. *My American Journey*. New York: Random House, 1995. 43

8. Howard Means. *Colin Powell*. New York: Random House, 1992. 106.

Chapter 4. Tour of Duty: Vietnam

1. Colin Powell and Joseph E. Persico. *My American Journey*. New York: Random House, 1995. 544.
2. Ibid. 85.
3. Ibid. 82.
4. Ibid. 94.
5. Ibid. 95.
6. John F. Kennedy. "Radio and Television Report to the American People on Civil Rights." *John F. Kennedy Presidential Library & Museum*. 11 June 1963. 6 Apr. 2009 <http://www.jfklibrary.org/ Historical+Resources/Archives/Reference+Desk/Speeches/ JFK/003POF03CivilRights06111963.htm>.

Chapter 5. A Master's and a Fellowship

1. Colin Powell and Joseph E. Persico. *My American Journey*. New York: Random House, 1995. 154.
2. Ibid. 157.
3. "White House Fellows." *The White House*. 7 Apr. 2009 <http:// www.whitehouse.gov/about/fellows/>.
4. Ibid.
5. "Colin Powell: A Soldier Turned Diplomat Faces New War on Terrorism." *People in the News*. *CNN.com*. 2004. 7 Apr. 2009 <http:// www.cnn.com/CNN/Programs/people/shows/powell/profile.html>.

Source Notes Continued

Chapter 6. White House General
1. Colin Powell and Joseph E. Persico. *My American Journey*. New York: Random House, 1995. 177.
2. Ibid. 196.
3. Ibid. 234.
4. Ibid. 243.
5. Ibid. 301.
6. Ronald Reagan. "Address to the Nation on the Iran Arms and Contra Aid Controversy." *Ronald Reagan Presidential Foundation*. 4 Mar. 1987. 8 Apr. 2009 <http://www.reagan.utexas.edu/archives/speeches/1987/030487h.htm>.

Chapter 7. Up the Political Ladder
1. Oren Harari. "Quotations from Chairman Powell: A Leadership Primer." *GovLeaders.org*. 1996. 8 Apr. 2009 <http://www.govleaders.org/powell.htm>.
2. Howard Means. *Colin Powell: A Biography*. New York: Random House, 1992. 253.
3. Colin L. Powell. "US Forces: Challenges Ahead." *Foreign Affairs*. Winter 1992. 8 Apr. 2009 <http://www.pbs.org/wgbh/pages/frontline/shows/military/force/powell.html>.
4. Ibid.
5. Ibid.

Chapter 8. Civilian Life
1. Colin Powell and Joseph E. Persico. *My American Journey*. New York: Random House, 1995. 554.
2. Ibid. 591.

Chapter 9. Secretary of State
1. "Colin Powell: A Soldier Turned Diplomat Faces New War on Terrorism." *People in the News*. *CNN.com*. 2004. 7 Apr. 2009 <http://www.cnn.com/CNN/Programs/people/shows/powell/profile.html>.
2. Colin L. Powell. "Key Policy Statements." *Benjamin Franklin Library*. 18 Jan. 2002. 13 Apr. 2009 <http://www.usembassy-mexico.gov/bbf/bfdossier_Terrorismo.htm>.
3. Colin Powell. "Transcript of Powell's U.N. Presentation." *CNN. com*. 5 Feb. 2003. 13 Apr. 2009 <http://www.cnn.com/2003/US/02/05/sprj.irq.powell.transcript.05/index.html>.
4. Ibid.
5. "Powell Calls Pre-Iraq U.N. Speech a 'Blot' on His Record." *USA Today*. 8 Sept. 2005. 13 Apr. 2009 <http://www.usatoday.com/news/washington/2005-09-08-powell-iraq_x.htm>.
6. Karen DeYoung. *Soldier: The Life of Colin Powell*. New York: Random House, 2006. 520.

INDEX

ABOUT THE AUTHOR

Sue Vander Hook has been writing and editing books for more than 15 years. Although her writing career began with several nonfiction books for adults, Vander Hook's main focus is educational books for children and young adults. She especially enjoys writing about historical events and biographies of people who made a difference. Her published works also include a high school curriculum and several series on disease, technology, and sports. Vander Hook lives with her family in Minnesota.

PHOTO CREDITS

Elizabeth Dalziel/AP Images, cover; Rick Maiman/Sygma/Corbis, 6, 14, 19, 23, 24, 33, 55, 59; AP Images, 9, 43, 44, 66, 96; Ron Edmonds/AP Images, 13, 69, 76; Horst Faas/AP Images, 34, 49, 97 (top), 97 (bottom); Rolls Press/Popperfoto/Getty Images, 39; Marie Mathelin/Roger Viollet/Getty Images, 56; Adele Starr/AP Images, 65, 98 (top); J. Scott Applewhite/AP Images, 75; Dennis Cook/AP Images, 85; Doug Mills/AP Images, 80, 86, 98 (bottom), 99; Elise Amendola/AP Images, 90; Haraz N. Ghanbari/AP Images, 95